PIANO
Adventures®

Challenging pieces with changing moods and changing hand positions

by Nancy and Randall Faber

THE BASIC PIANO METHOD

Production Coordinator: Jon Ophoff
Design and Illustration: Terpstra Design, San Francisco

FABER
PIANO ADVENTURES®

ISBN 978-1-61677-603-9

Table of Contents

("Gold Star" characteristics of each piece)
Color the star gold or put a star sticker for each piece you learn!

FF1603

Most of All I Like Rainbows

Words by Crystal Bowman
Music by Nancy Faber

Teacher Duet: (Student plays 1 octave higher, without pedal)

FF160

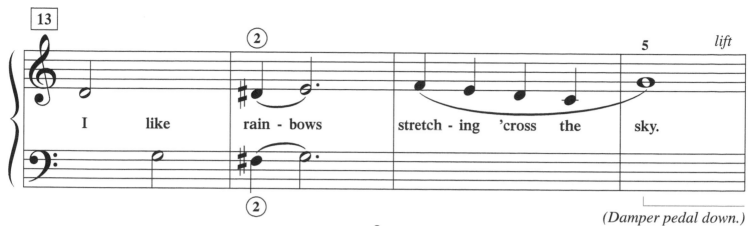

13

I like rain-bows stretch-ing 'cross the sky.

(Damper pedal down.)

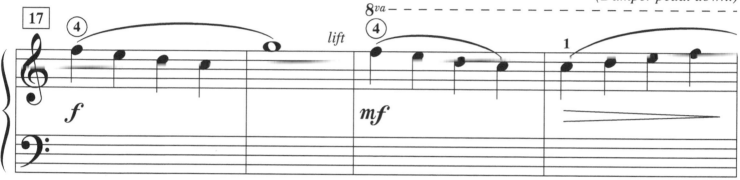

17

f

lift

8va

mf

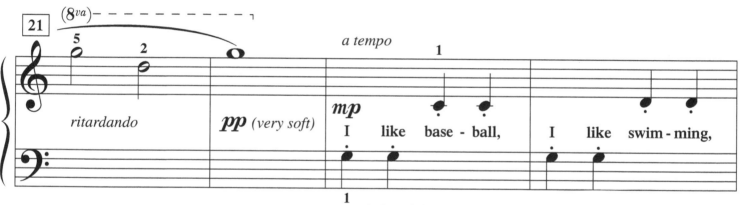

21

(8va)

ritardando

pp (very soft)

a tempo

mp

I like base-ball, I like swim-ming,

(Lift pedal.)

25

I like sand be-tween my toes. But what I like most of all:

L.H. ② *over*

f

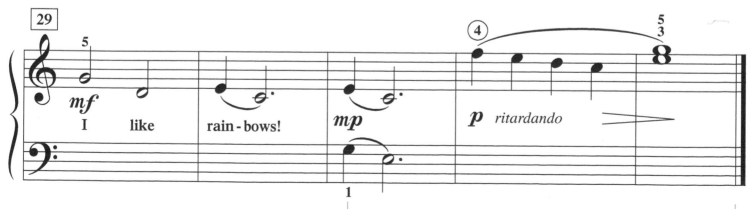

29

mf

I like rain-bows!

mp

p ritardando

Bullfrog Blues

Words and Music
by Nancy Faber

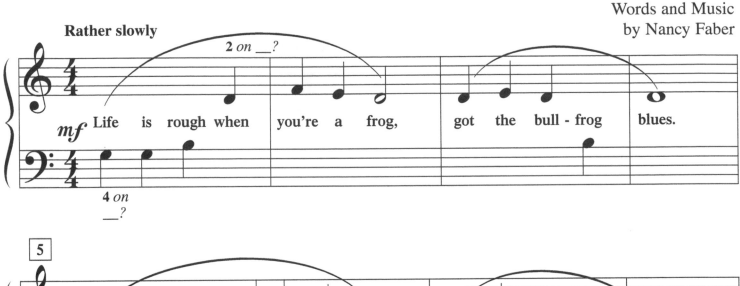

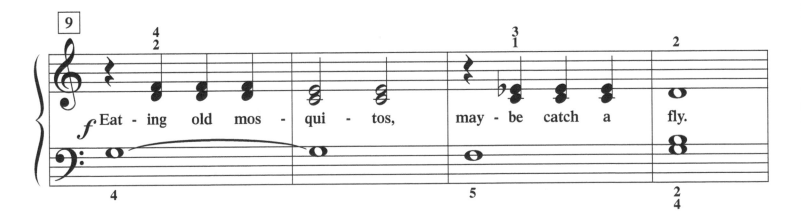

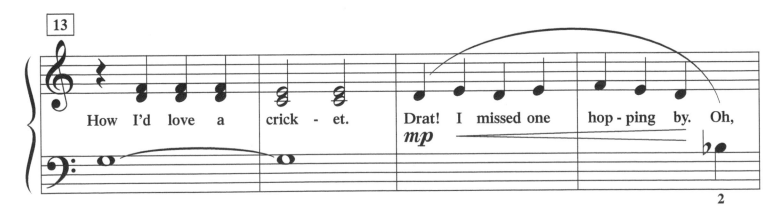

FF1603

17 *mf* life is tough when you're a frog, got the bull - frog blues.

4

21 Days and weeks up - on this log, got the bull - frog blues. *Move both hands 8va lower.*

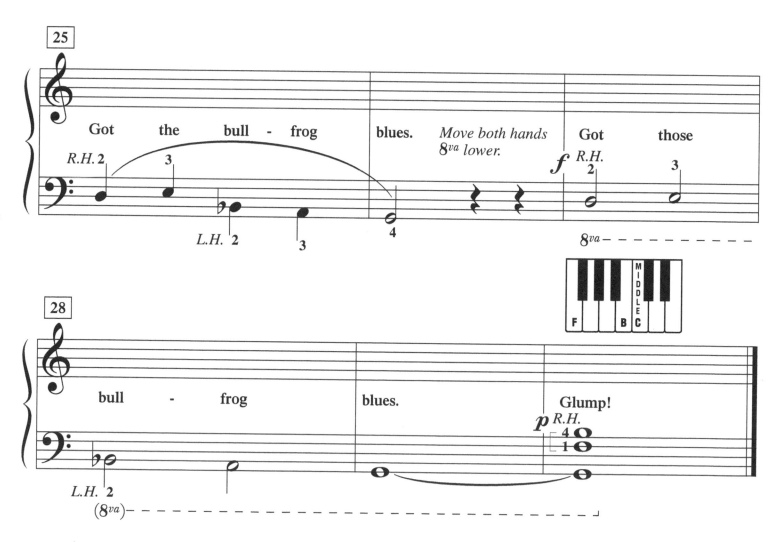

25 Got the bull - frog blues. *Move both hands 8va lower.* Got those

R.H. 2 *3* *L.H. 2* *3* *4* *f R.H. 2* *3*

8va – – – – – – – – –

28 bull - frog blues. Glump!

p R.H. 4 1

L.H. 2

(8va) – – – – – – – – – – –

DISCOVERY

Name the two **flats** used in this piece.

Monster's Midnight March

**Play BOTH HANDS in the
LOWEST D Positions
(all white keys) on the piano.**

Nancy Faber

Marching strongly

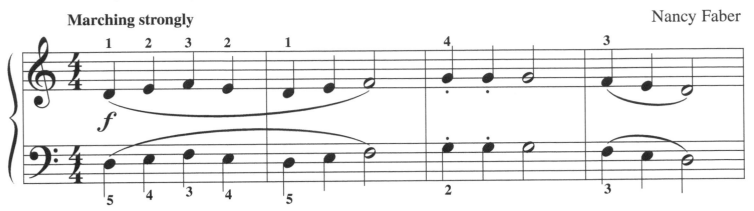

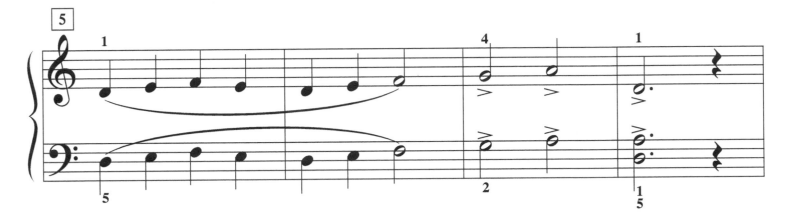

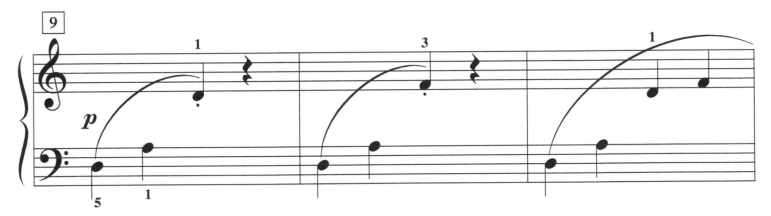

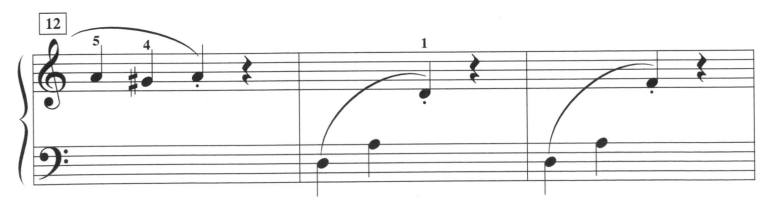

FF160

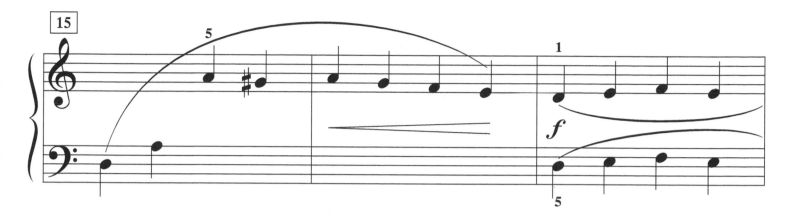

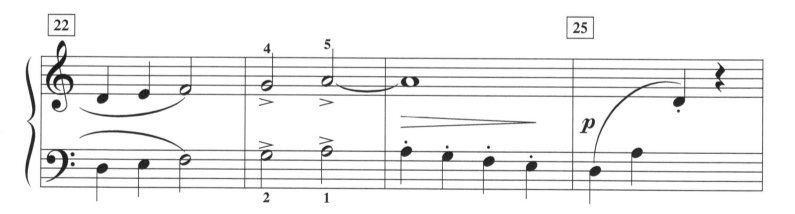

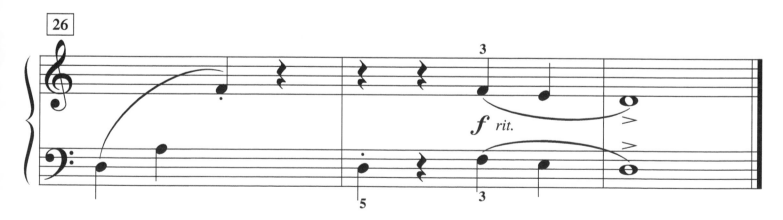

DISCOVERY

Where does the opening melody return in the piece? Tell your teacher.

Colorful Sonatina

1. Sunshine Yellow

Nancy Faber

Happily, "in two"

Teacher Duet: (Student plays 1 octave higher)

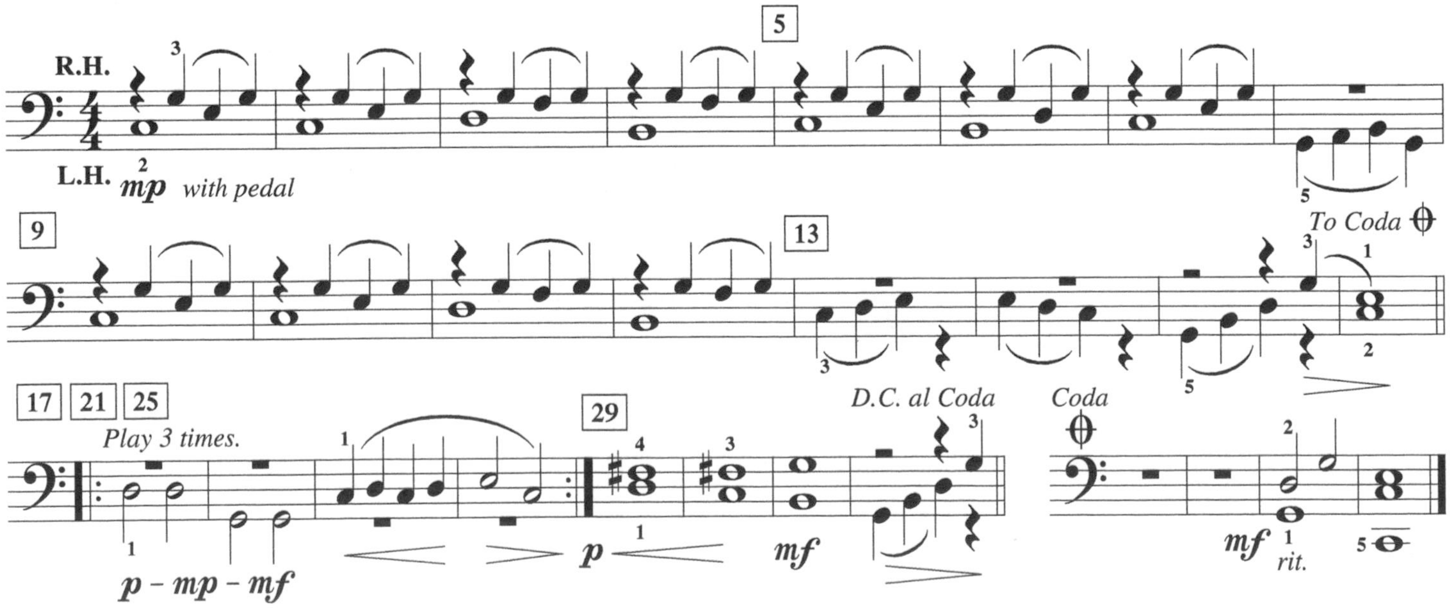

FF160

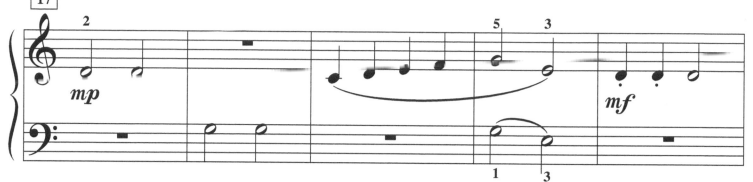

D.C. al Coda

Coda

DISCOVERY The organization of a piece is called musical form.
The form of this piece is **A B A** *coda* (ending).
Your teacher will help you label each section.

2. Dreamy Sky Blue

Moving gently

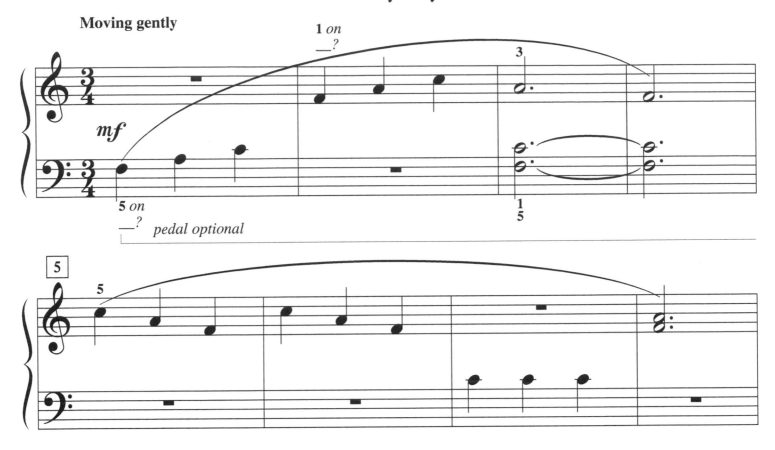

Teacher Duet: (Student plays 1 octave higher, without pedal)

FF160

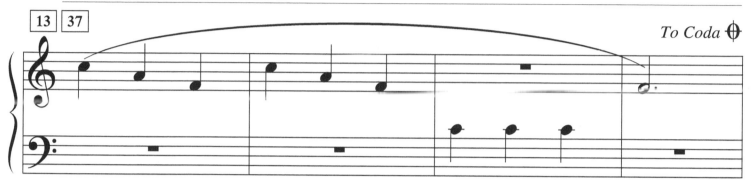

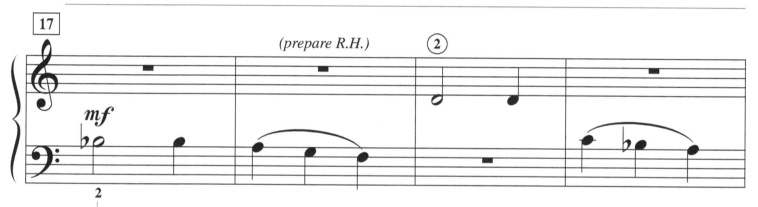

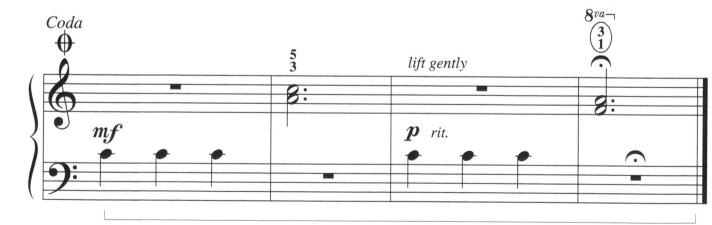

This form is also **A B A** *coda*. Can you find and label the sections?

3. Happy Red

FF1603

move quickly!

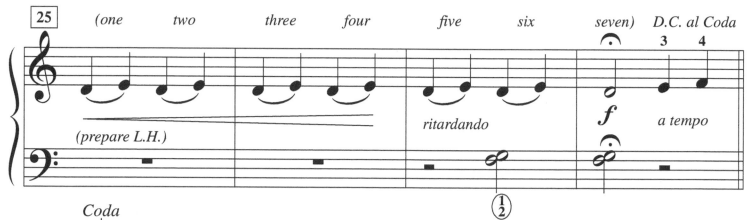

Canoe Song

Traditional Words
Arranged by Nancy Faber

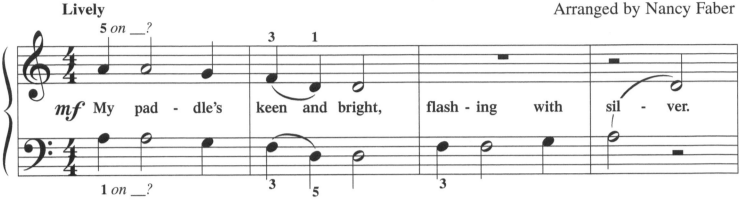

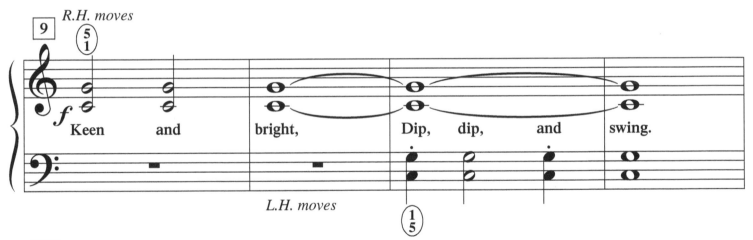

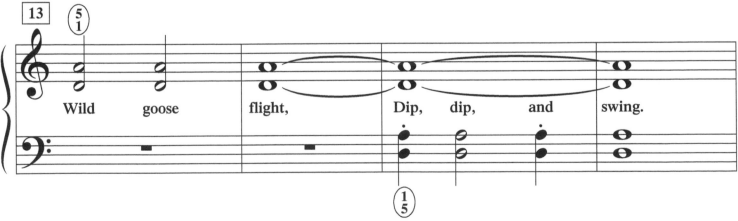

FF160

17

p Pale sun - light, Dip, dip, and swing.

21

(prepare L.H.)

25

f My pad - dle's keen and bright, flash - ing with sil - ver.

29

Fol - low the wild goose flight, dip, dip, and swing.

33

p Dip, dip, and swing. Dip, dip, and swing. *Cross R.H. over L.H. to lowest D!*

8ᵛᵃ- - - - - -

DISCOVERY

Point out the following: **slur**, *staccato*, the interval of a *5th*, *tie*, *8ᵛᵃ* sign.

Happiness Runs
Secondo

Play BOTH HANDS *8ᵛᵃ* **LOWER**
throughout the piece.

Traditional words and melody
Arranged by Nancy Faber

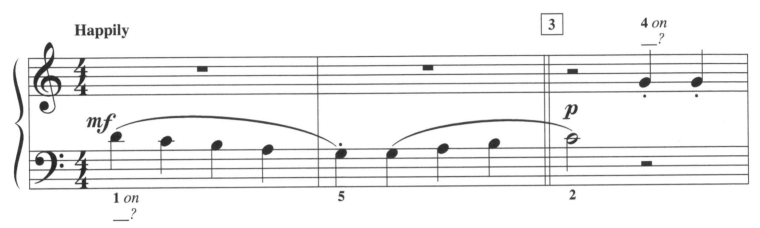

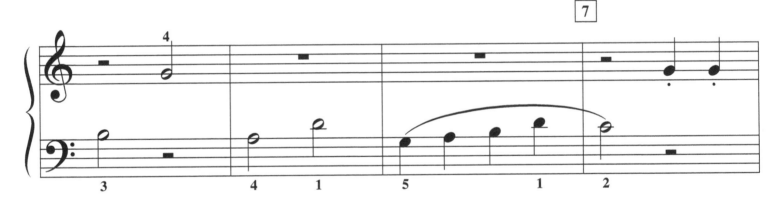

FF160

Happiness Runs
Primo

Play BOTH HANDS *8va* **HIGHER throughout the piece.**

Traditional words and melody
Arranged by Nancy Faber

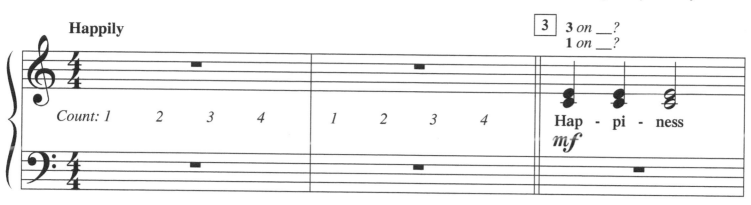

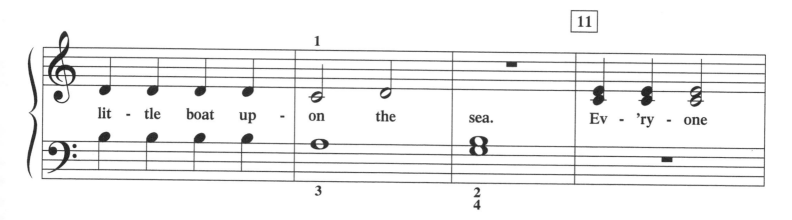

Secondo

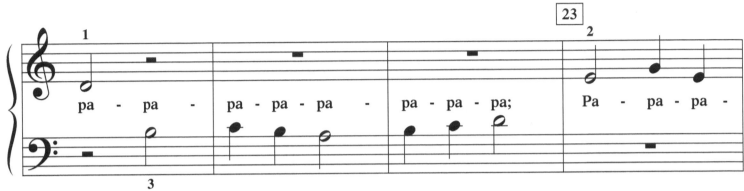

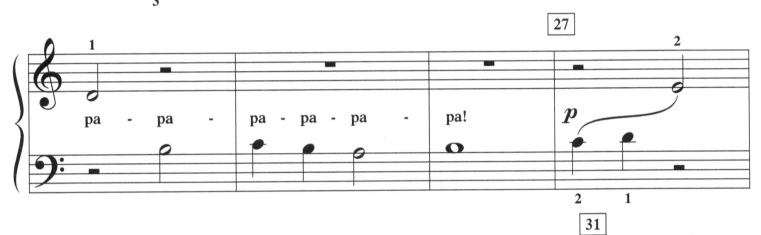

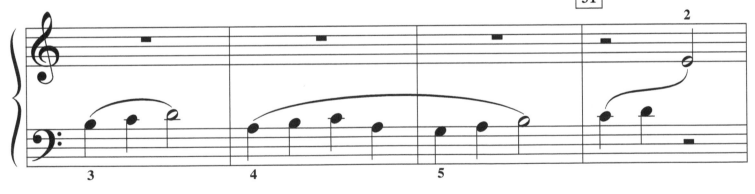

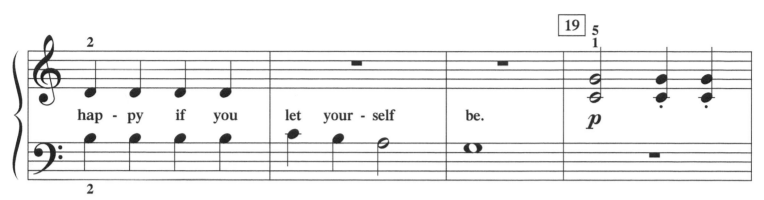

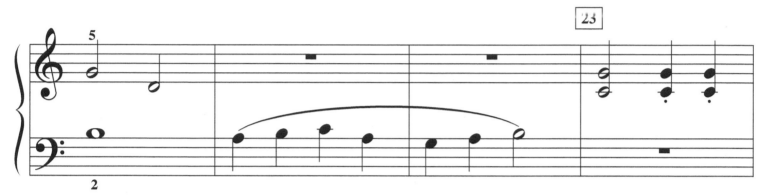

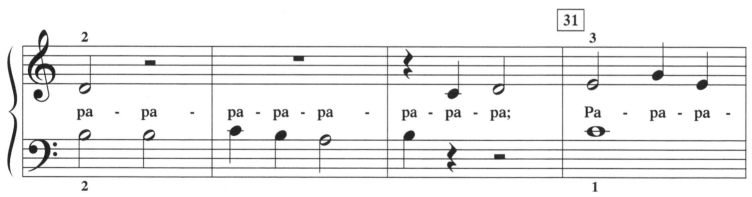

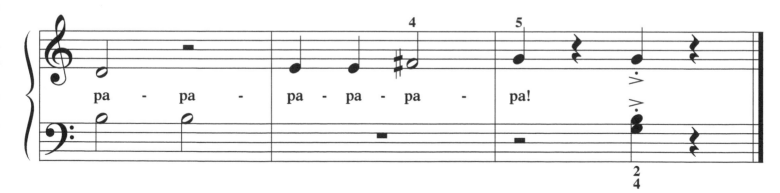

Chinese Painting

**Hold the damper pedal down
throughout the piece.**

Traditional Chinese Melody
Arranged by Nancy Faber

Flowing smoothly

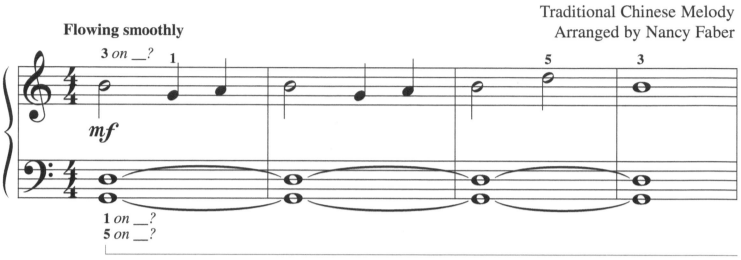

Pedal down.

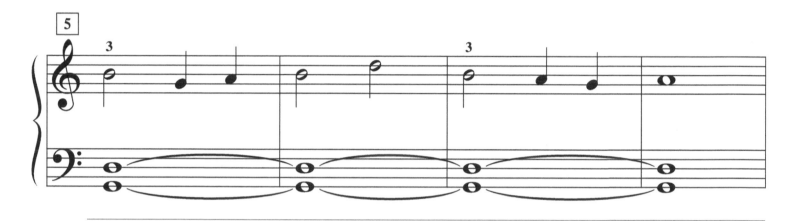

FF1603

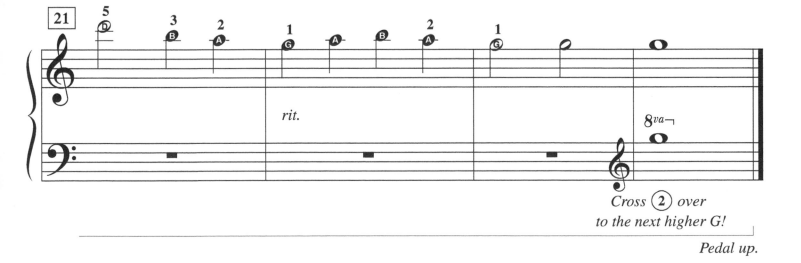

Pedal up.

* Note to Teacher: Encourage students to read these notes directionally.

DISCOVERY

Play *measures 1–16* with the right hand *8va* higher.

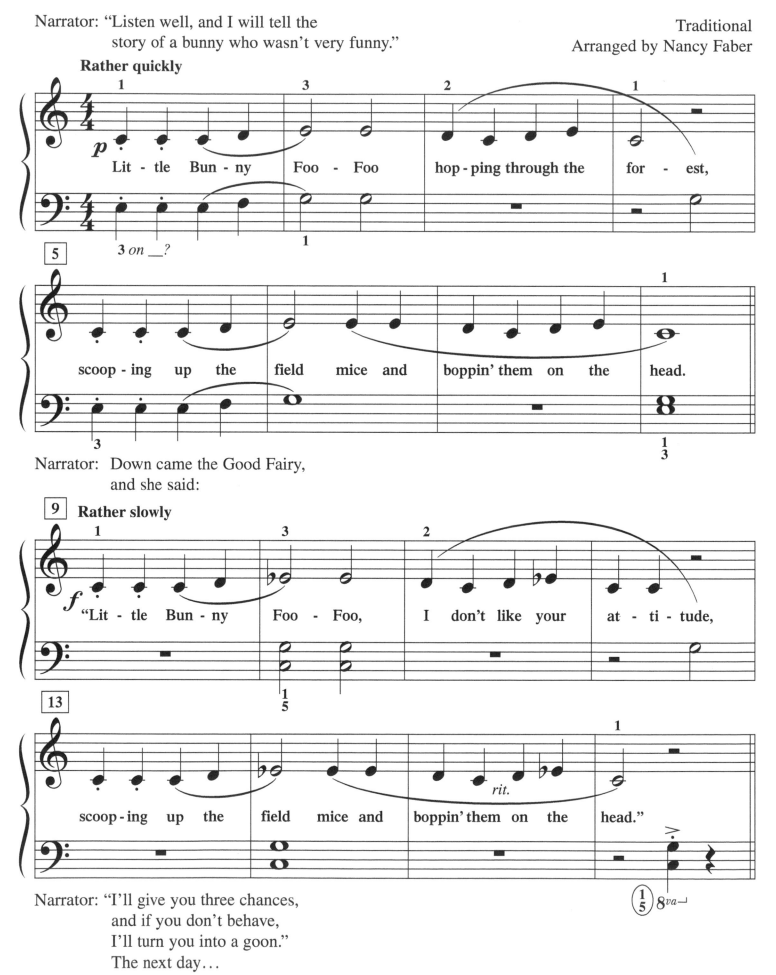

Little Bunny Foo Foo

Narrator: "Listen well, and I will tell the
story of a bunny who wasn't very funny."

Traditional
Arranged by Nancy Faber

Rather quickly

Lit - tle Bun - ny Foo - Foo hop - ping through the for - est,

3 *on ___*?

scoop - ing up the field mice and boppin' them on the head.

Narrator: Down came the Good Fairy,
and she said:

Rather slowly

"Lit - tle Bun - ny Foo - Foo, I don't like your at - ti - tude,

scoop - ing up the field mice and boppin' them on the head."

rit.

Narrator: "I'll give you three chances,
and if you don't behave,
I'll turn you into a goon."
The next day…

G 5-Finger Position

17 Rather quickly

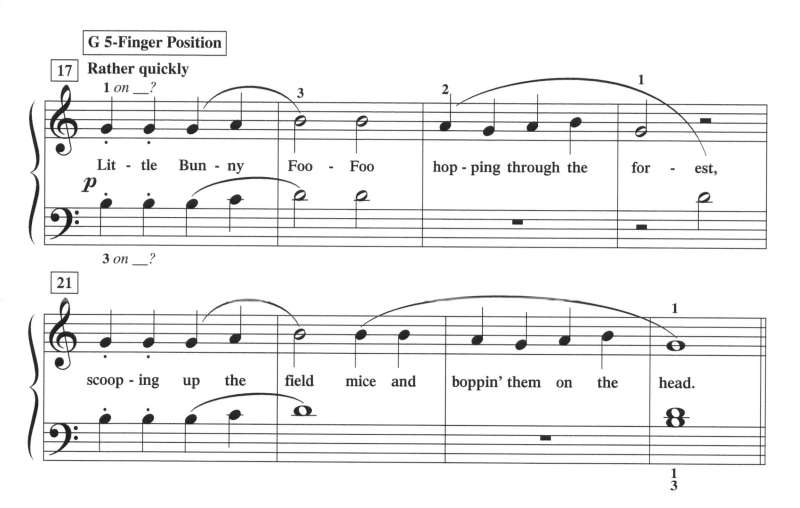

Lit - tle Bun - ny Foo - Foo hop - ping through the for - est,

3 on __?

21

scoop - ing up the field mice and boppin' them on the head.

Narrator: Down came the Good Fairy,
and she said:

25 Rather slowly

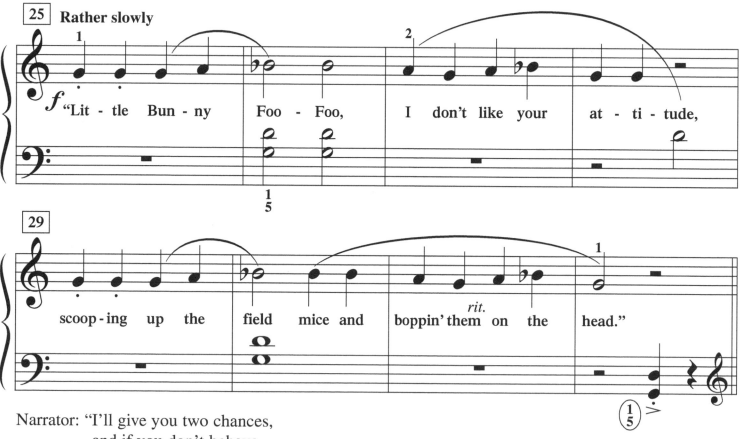

f "Lit - tle Bun - ny Foo - Foo, I don't like your at - ti - tude,

29

scoop - ing up the field mice and boppin' them on the head."

Narrator: "I'll give you two chances,
and if you don't behave,
I'll turn you into a goon."
The next day…

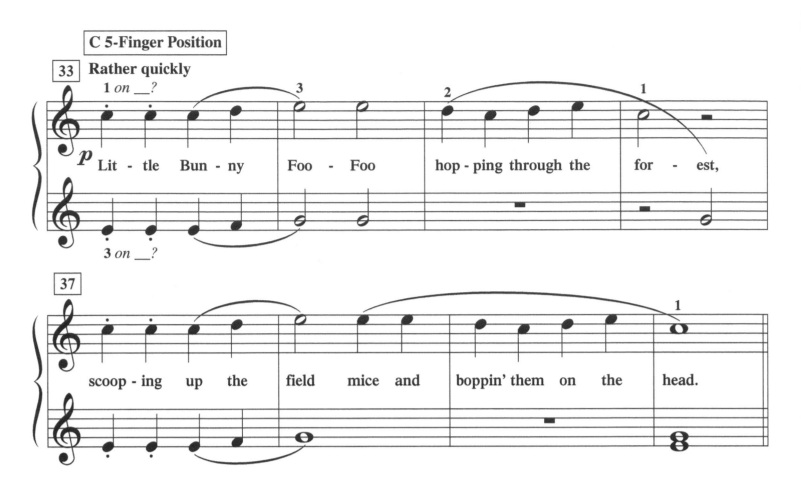

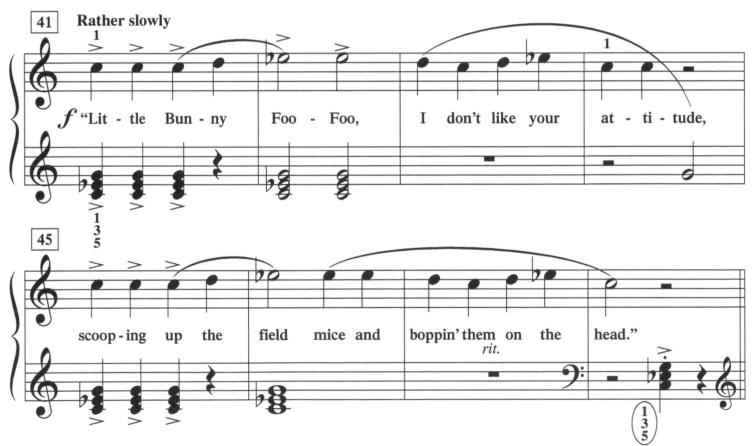

Narrator: Down came the Good Fairy,
and she said:

Narrator: "I'll give you one more chance,
and if you don't behave,
I'll turn you into a goon."
The next day...

Rather quickly

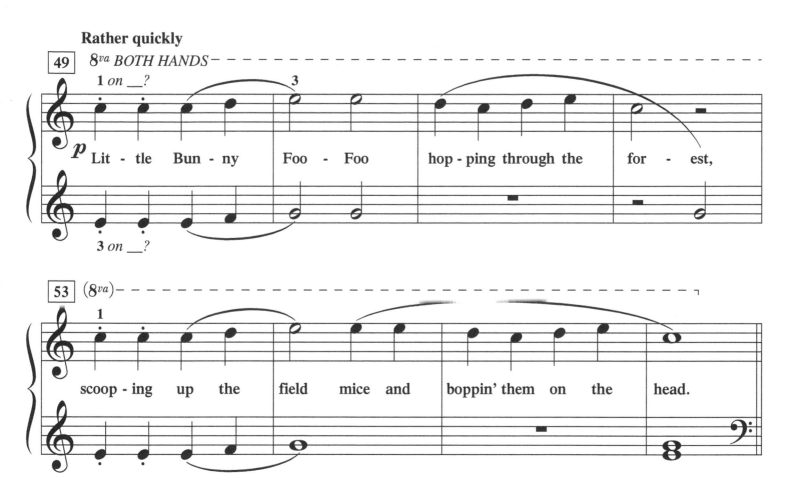

49 8va BOTH HANDS — — — — — —

p Lit - tle Bun - ny Foo - Foo hop - ping through the for - est,

53 (8va) — — — — —

scoop - ing up the field mice and boppin' them on the head.

Narrator: Down came the Good Fairy,
and she said:
"I gave you three chances,
and you didn't behave.
Now, I'll turn you into a goon!"

f
POOF!

(Play all
5 fingers
together.)

Narrator: The moral of the story is:
HARE TODAY, GOON TOMORROW!

57 **Slowly**

*Play the lowest C
on the piano!*

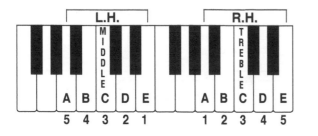

Haiku

Music by Nancy Faber
Poem by Matsuo Basho
(1644–1694)

Play BOTH HANDS 8va **higher throughout the piece.**

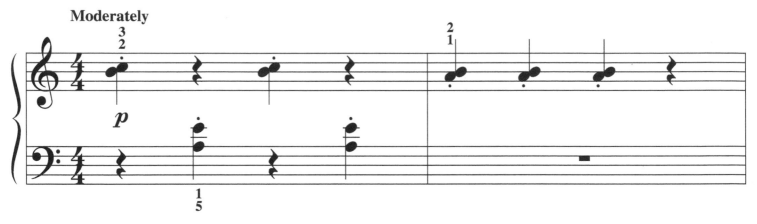

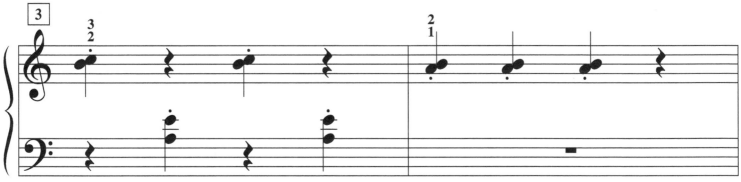

Haiku: *The old pond —*

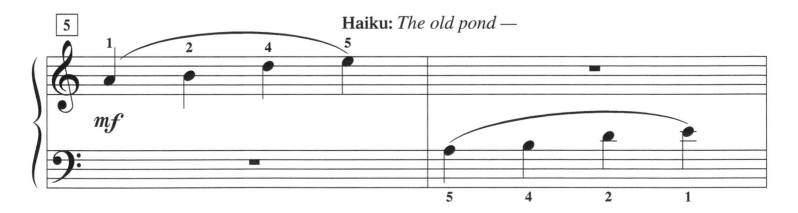

a frog jumps in:

FF1603

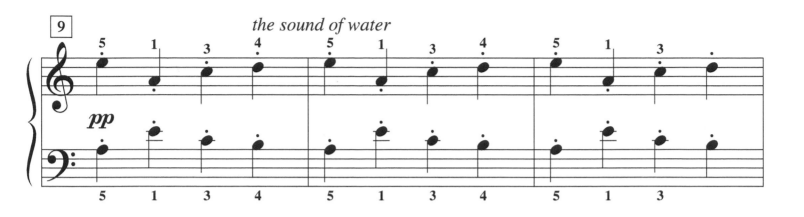

the sound of water

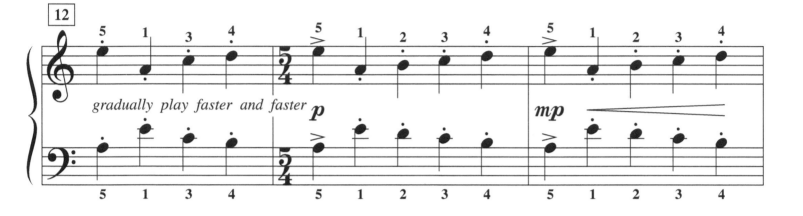

gradually play faster and faster

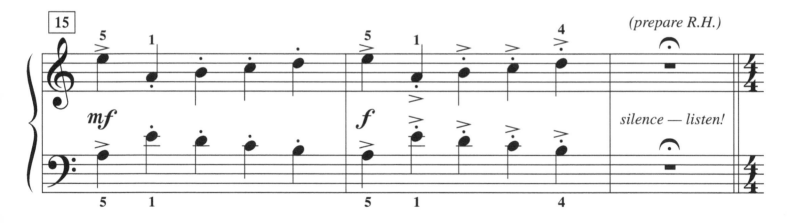

(prepare R.H.)

silence — listen!

Keep rounded
hands in air
as if holding
the silence.

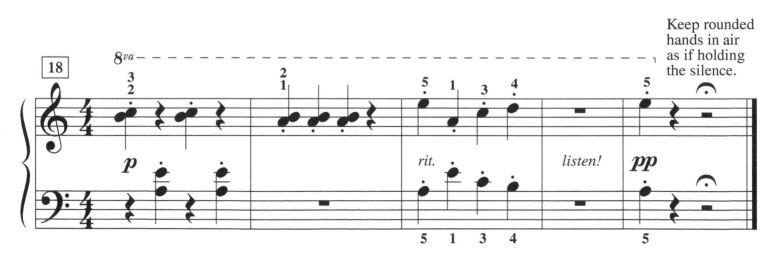

rit.

listen!

Dance of Two Seahorses*
(from *First Instruction in Piano-Playing*)

Carl Czerny
(1791–1857, Austria)
original form

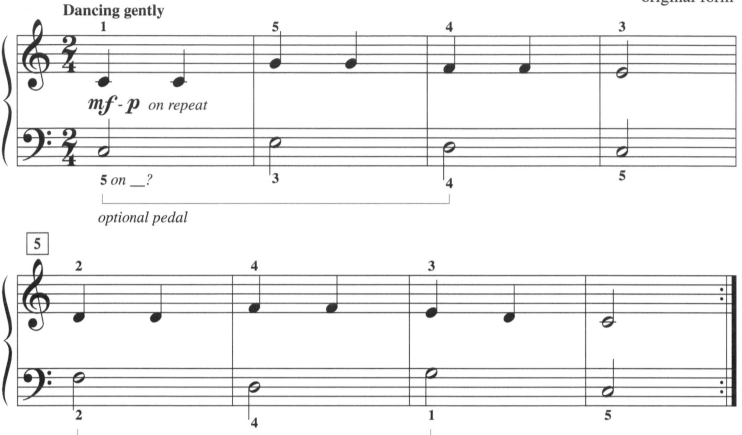

Dancing gently

mf - p on repeat

5 on __?

optional pedal

*originally written one octave higher

Teacher Duet: (Student plays 1 octave higher, without pedal)

Duet by the authors

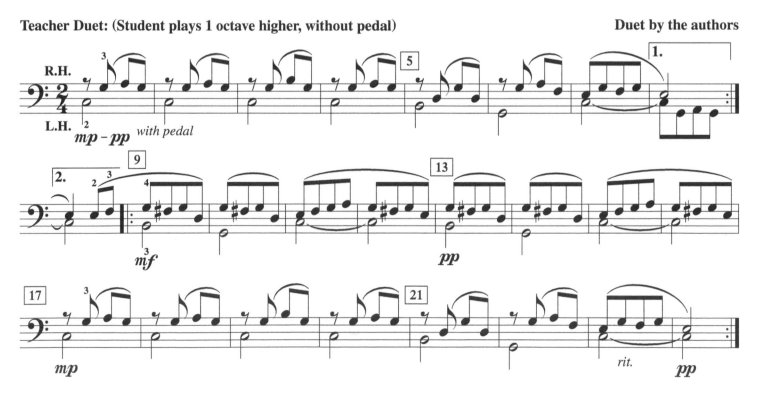

FF1603

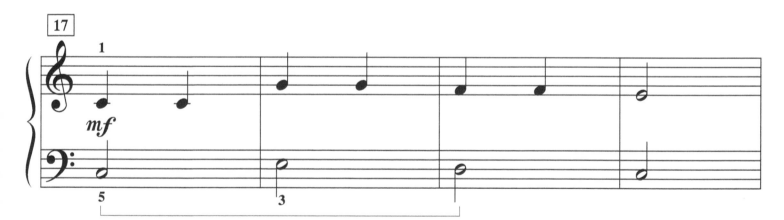

DISCOVERY

What is the only rhythm used by the left hand? *(circle one)*
quarter note   half note   whole note

Mouses or Meese

Words by Crystal Bowman
Music by Nancy Faber

Move L.H. to the
C 5-finger scale.

FF1603

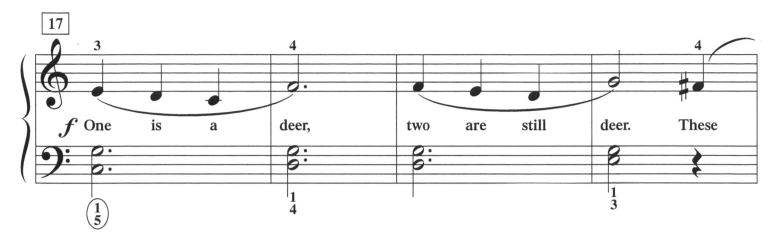

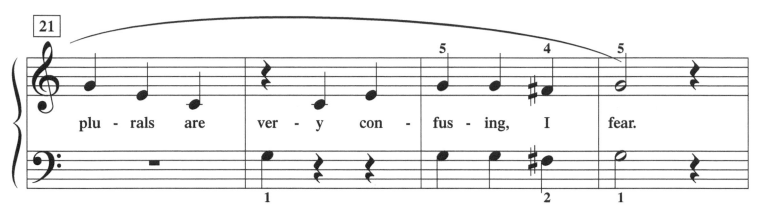

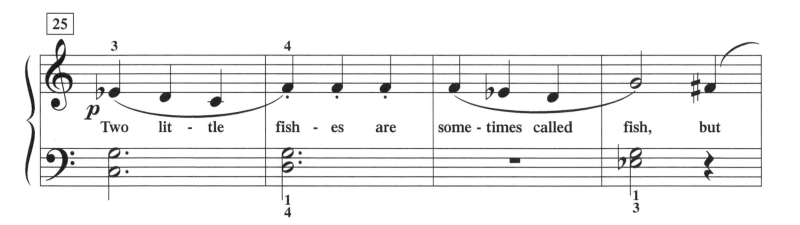

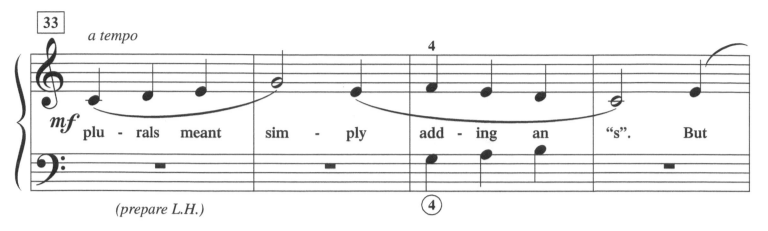

33 *a tempo*

mf plu - rals meant sim - ply add - ing an "s". But

(prepare L.H.)

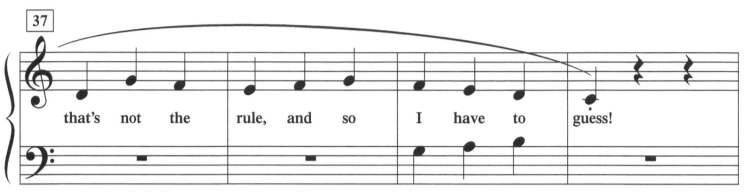

37

that's not the rule, and so I have to guess!

Move L.H. 1 octave lower

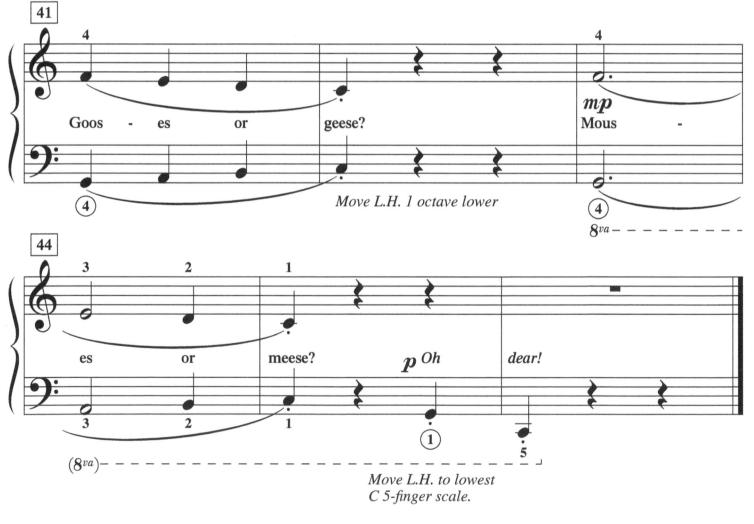

41

Goos - es or geese? Mous -

Move L.H. 1 octave lower

8va - - - - - - - - -

44

es or meese? *p* Oh dear!

(8va) - - - - - - - - -

*Move L.H. to lowest
C 5-finger scale.*

DISCOVERY Can you think of an animal and its plural?

Three Pirates

Traditional Words
Music by Nancy Faber

FF1603

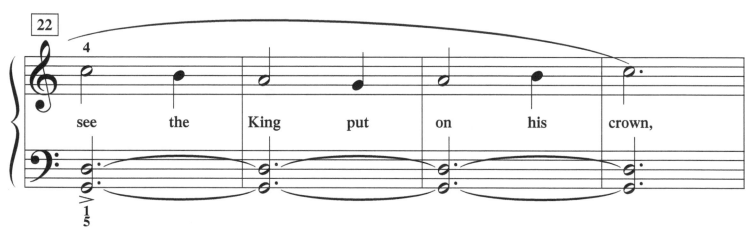

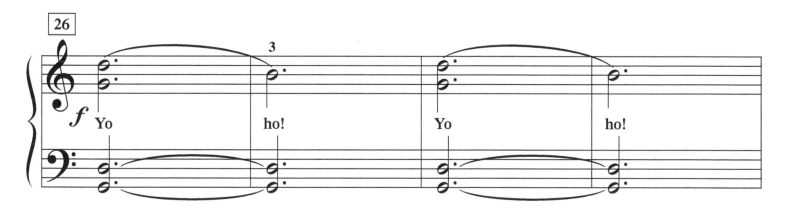

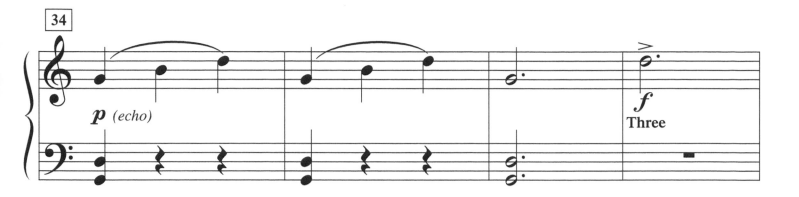

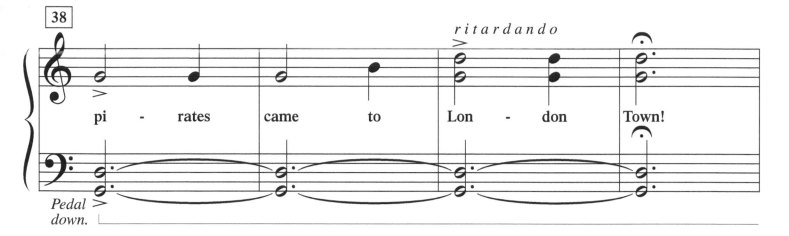

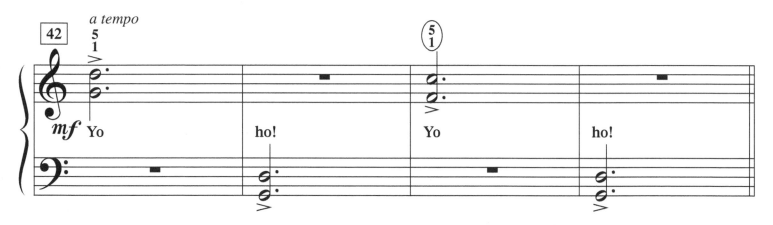

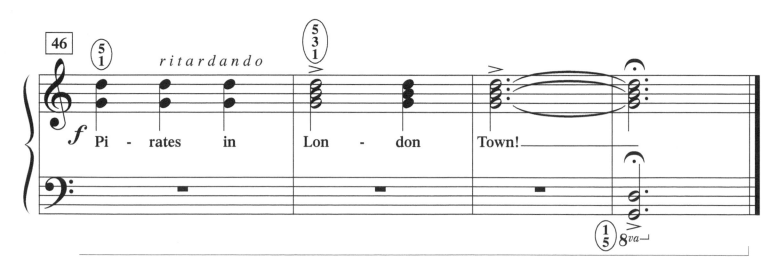

DISCOVERY

What interval is used from *measure 42* to *measure 46*?

Gold Star Dictionary

Circle a gold star when you can pronounce each term and tell your teacher what it means!

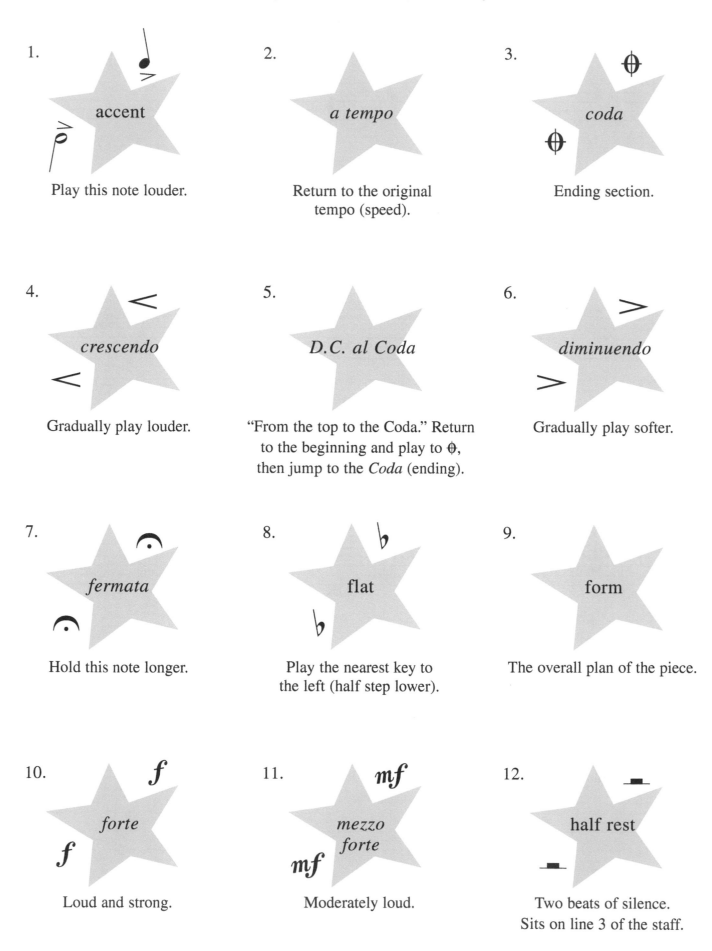

1. **accent** — Play this note louder.

2. **a tempo** — Return to the original tempo (speed).

3. **coda** — Ending section.

4. **crescendo** — Gradually play louder.

5. **D.C. al Coda** — "From the top to the Coda." Return to the beginning and play to ⊕, then jump to the *Coda* (ending).

6. **diminuendo** — Gradually play softer.

7. **fermata** — Hold this note longer.

8. **flat** — Play the nearest key to the left (half step lower).

9. **form** — The overall plan of the piece.

10. **forte** — Loud and strong.

11. **mezzo forte** — Moderately loud.

12. **half rest** — Two beats of silence. Sits on line 3 of the staff.

FF160

13. *mp* **mp** *mezzo piano*

Moderately soft.

14. 8va *ottava* 8va

Play 1 octave higher or lower than written.

15. *pp* **pp** *pianissimo*

Very softly.

16. *p* **p** *piano*

Softly, gently.

17. *primo*

The higher part in a 4-hand duet.

18. *quarter rest*

1 beat of silence.
Count: 1

19. *rit.* *ritardando* *ritard.*

Gradually play slower.

20. *secondo*

The lower part in a 4-hand duet.

21. *sharp*

Play the nearest key to the right (half step higher).

22. *slur*

Connect the notes over or under a slur.

23. *staccato*

Play staccato notes detached.

24. *tie*

A curved line connecting the same notes. Hold for the total counts of both notes.

25. $\frac{4}{4}$ *time signature* $\frac{3}{4}$ $\frac{2}{4}$

Top number shows the number of beats per measure. Lower number shows the quarter note gets 1 beat.

26. *whole rest*

Four beats of silence. Hangs below line 4 of the staff. Used for any whole measure.

GOLD STAR CERTIFICATE

CONGRATULATIONS,
Gold Star Performer!

You have completed the Piano Adventures
Gold Star Performance, Level 1.

You are now ready to begin
Gold Star Performance, Level 2A.

Write your name in the star to celebrate your progress!